THE POWER OF LEADERSHIP

THE POWER OF LEADERSHIP

BY
MARCUS D. DAVIDSON
&
FRANK KENNEDY JR.

To Cameron
Your Life is schedule For greatnus.
Remember: Failvre is the face of your
Future in refinement.
Grace & peace   Soli Deo
PS. 37:4   Gloria!
FK GK—

XULON PRESS

Xulon Press
2301 Lucien Way #415
Maitland, FL 32751
407.339.4217
www.xulonpress.com

Edited by Xulon Press.

Printed in the United States of America.

ISBN-13: 978-1-54563-331-1

ACKNOWLEDGEMENTS

Marcus Davidson:

First and foremost, I would like to thank my wife Yvokia for encouraging me in this journey of ministry and writing this book. I would also like to thank my daughter, Layla for constantly telling me how she is excited about Daddy writing a book. I would like to thank my parents, siblings, and in-laws for always supporting and praying for me. I would like to thank my staff and congregation of the New Mount Olive Baptist Church for their unfailing support of all of my endeavors to excel. I would like to thank Michele Roberts for consistent support through this writing journey. Finally, I thank my friend and brother in ministry, Frank Kennedy Jr. for partnering with me in ministry for the Gory of God. *Soli Deo Gloria*!

Frank Kennedy, Jr.

I am profoundly grateful for the contributions of many persons who have supported and influenced my vocational pilgrimage. I would like to thank my wife Denise for her sacrificial support and sustaining belief that God would use my life and ministry for His glory. To my phenomenal daughters, Cierro and Lachastity, thanks for your incessant encouragement and motivation regardless of the rigors of life and ministry.

I would like to thank my mother Geneva and my father Frank Sr., for their nurturing love and tremendous support of my varied vocational transitions. To the New Mount Olive Baptist Church, thank you for your lovingkindness and exceptional encouragement. My pastor and partner in kingdom labor, Dr. Marcus D. Davidson; words seem so inadequate, when I think of the abundance of grace provided me to work in kingdom style with such a man of God. Thank you for trusting God and me, His servant. *Soli Deo Gloria*!

TABLE OF CONTENTS

FOREWORD

M any books have been published on leadership—both secular and sacred. Many authors have integrated both the secular and biblical aspects of leadership in their particular books. Here is another book on leadership that I believe you will want to add to your library.

In "The Power of Leadership", Pastor Marcus Davidson and Pastor Frank Kennedy Jr. have given some practical, profound, and personal reflections on how to be a faithful and effective servant leader. Both men have had solid pastoral experience grounded in sound theological studies and practice. They both understand that one of the most important aspects of being a fruitful and faithful leader is to be sure that God has called you to lovingly lead His people. In fact, the success of all real pastoral leaders is anchored in their assurance that they have the authority and presence of God undergirding and guiding their leadership call and response. Consequently when tough times and difficult days arise in the life of a pastor's leadership roles, he has sufficient power to manage and move forward because he has God's promise that His grace is sufficient for you and His strength is made perfect in weakness (I Corinthians 12:9).

The authors of this book have carefully woven together from the opening chapter on "The Power of Prayer" to the closing chapter on "The Power of Planning", that God's power and guidance must fuel every phrase, every sentence, every paragraph, and every chapter of the of the pastor's life as he seeks to lead God's people. And perhaps most important of all, the successful leader will always shape his/her vision and chart his/her course baptized in the priority of prayer, because prayer flows to and from the heart of God.

Julius R. Scruggs, Pastor
First Missionary Baptist Church
Huntsville, AL
Past President of the National Baptist
Convention, USA, Inc.

INTRODUCTION

This introduction to the Power of Leadership is, in no way, meant to deter you from your desire to be a leader. However, it would not be fair to not offer a disclaimer to all the lofty accolades entailed in leadership that are included in this book. Being a leader can give you a sense of pride and accomplishment, but there will be times of darkroom despair that your audience will never see. When the low times come, recall your reason for wanting to lead.

The scripture verse of Matthew 9:37 that says the harvest is ripe and the workers are few is an admonishment to leaders for allowing people/sheep to be scattered as they sat dormant. There is plenty of work to be done, for all souls are not yet saved. This same sentiment of lost sheep is still a reality today; many are wandering in search of a word for their hurting hearts. It is commendable to want to lead God's people; for it is most likely a call deep in your heart from God, and an answer to those looking for guidance. As a gifted leader, you cannot see people wandering in hopelessness and not be filled with compassion to help them. God chooses you wisely; the harvest of souls is more ready now and workers are desperately needed.

Matthew 14:26-29 says this:

---

[26] If anyone comes to Me, and does not hate his own father and mother and wife and children and brothers and sisters, yes, and even his own life, he cannot be My disciple. [27] Whoever does not carry his own cross and come after Me cannot be My disciple. [28] For which one of you, when he wants to build a tower, does not first sit down and calculate the cost to see if he has enough to complete it? [29] Otherwise, when he has laid a foundation and is not able to finish, all who observe it begin to ridicule him...."

This passage is a word to all believers who are being converted from entirely different lifestyles. If these words are for anyone who has decided to become a believer, where does that leave those desiring to be leaders of these believers? Surely you have to be prepared for the step-up. Your excuses for falling short of completing your tasks may fly as a member of the usher board or the second alto on the mass choir, but not so much as the pastor, assistant pastor or anyone of the many team leader positions needed to form ministry. You are required, and should be prepared, to do more than the masses you have chosen to lead.

Matthew 14:26, the verse above, actually says that you must choose to hate your own family. Of course hate here is a very strong word, but it is exactly what Jesus intended. Many may choose leadership with no thought of the challenges that they will face. You can be a sheep needing guidance and take your time developing when guidance is given, but as a leader, your learning curve must be alleviated quickly, and with as little distraction as possible. You will not treat your spouse or any family member poorly, but your relationship must be in proper perspective. Just as Abraham obeyed God and was prepared to sacrifice his promised son, Isaac, this is the sentiment that Jesus wants from His followers. Abraham loved his son, but had to choose to "hate" him in order to prove his faith to God. God loves family and did not allow Abraham to kill his son of promise. Your family is just as important to God, as was the life of Abraham's son, but God comes first.

You are reading this, which means that you are ready to take the first step into leadership. You have calculated the expense of your choice. You have lined up your life to coincide with what you may have to do. In this book, there are scriptural examples as well as contemporary thoughts on leadership. Many of the principles in this book have already been applied to your life; some may need upgrading. The idea of enabling assistants and springing into action when the needs of people are presented are both leadership attributes. As one being led you can stand and watch others work, but your action hat must be worn all the time as a leader. Everyone that grows must continue to learn; continue to learn and grow, and your leadership ability will be phenomenal.

Remain focused and allow God to be your ultimate guide. You are guaranteed to be successful, so decide that you will stay the course and not allow distractions to deter your work for God's Kingdom. You have been chosen and equipped. Keep your eye on the Great Shepherd of all the sheep, including you: Jesus Christ the Lord and Savior. He is willing and more than able to direct you to your destiny.

Chapter One

THE POWER OF PRAYER

There is power in prayer and as a leader; your most beneficial means of success will be your personal prayer life. For many believers, the mention of prayer brings on feelings of boredom and hard work. The problem is not with prayer, but the understanding of its purpose. There is no right way for personal prayer with God. There are guidelines for prayer, but how and when you pray with these instructions is your business. Matthew 5:6-8 tells you to pray in secret and God will reward you openly. One other very important element is that you do not say the same thing over and over. Prayer is your communication with God: He not only hears you, but is waiting for you to talk to Him. Prayer with God should never be monotonous or rigid.

Leaders are charged with equipping their followers to have a closer walk with Christ, along with fulfilling the ministry of a unified body of believers. This may sound like an easy task, and it can be. Nothing God gives you to do is hard, but when you try in your own strength to do all that your ministry requires, you will soon find out that your strength is small. It is not because you are physically or mentally weak, but it is the fact that what you are dealing with in ministry is a spiritual thing. Prayer is spiritual; connecting with God is spiritual. Jesus died and rose just for you to have access to your Heavenly Father. It would not make sense for you to leave such a privilege unused. You are called by God to lead, and He desires for you to ask Him for direction on leading His people. Some of your followers may not be as spiritually mature as others, while some of them may be more mature than you.

Paul instructed Timothy not to back down from those following him because of his youth: "Let no one look down on your youthfulness, but *rather* in speech, conduct, love, faith *and* purity, show yourself an example of those who believe" (I Tim.

4:12, NASB). Timothy was young; that did not matter. You may have members that are older than you or have been walking with the Lord longer than you; that does not matter to God. You are the one for the job and you should strive to be an example. Your thoughts about your own maturity have nothing to do with God giving you leadership responsibilities. Your prayer life will keep you ahead as a leader. You may be as young as Timothy was to those he inspired or as old as Joshua entering the Promised Land. You are still THE one to lead!

The most important thing in your prayer life is the ability to stay humble. In Matthew 6, Jesus instructed believers not to come to Him with repetitious, wordy prayers. You use clichés in every-day conversations you have with people; it is the way of life. You use small talk with acquaintances every day, but there is no way to build a strong relationship with anyone just repeating the same words every time you are in his/her presence. If your prayer life regularly says, "Thank you for not letting me beg on the street like that man I saw today. He needs to work just like I do," or "I really did well as I normally do. I am so glad that I am not like that drug addict that does not take care of his children," then you need to better understand the kind of prayers that God wants to hear. God wants honesty and heartfelt words from you, and Jesus even gave an example to guide His disciples on how to pray. He already knows you and what you need. Are you humble enough to ask Him bread for today and to deliver you from evil?

Just like you have private conversations with your closest friends and relatives, Jesus instructed His followers to do the same about public prayers. You should not pray in public just to prove how much you please your Heavenly Father. The attention you garner from those who hear you will be your reward, while praying in secret also gives you public rewards. In Luke 18, you also see an example of what not to do in prayer, as a Jewish leader is praying about how much he fasts and pays tithes. His prayers are nothing more than bragging to God about all he does for Him. Then the example is given of a sinner beating his chest and bowing his head, asking to be forgiven for his sins, which is an example of the kind of prayers that God loves. As a leader, you will need God to help you, and the only way that you will ask for help is if you know that you need it. Only the humble will acknowledge that they are nothing without God. Your private requests will be rewarded with public displays of elevation and spiritual maturity.

The power of prayer is also evident when believers come with one heart and one voice, calling on a loving Savior. You see this power changing an entire nation when the Israelites prayed to God for deliverance from slavery in the book of Exodus 2:23. Once again, you see this power of unity in prayer, displayed on the day of Pentecost when the Holy Spirit first came to earth in Acts 2. What better way to unify the people you are leading than praying together?

You may not even be aware of how much more assistance you can have if you would just ask others to pray. Your motive in prayer must be to be empowered by God to complete your assignment. James 4:3 tells you that you are not receiving what you need because you are not asking for it; hence, you may not be receiving your answer because you are asking for the wrong reason. You must have a singleness of mind and cannot ask to prove something to other people or other leaders; that is confusing your human desires with the ones you should have to see God's will carried out on earth. If you are aware that answers can be found in prayer, then pray God's will over what you are doing and watch the manifestation.

As a leader, what you need most from God is His wisdom; wisdom is the proper application of knowledge. You can study leadership and watch other great leaders, but no matter how prepared you may believe you are, trials are going to come. When they do, your best weapon will be your prayer life, and your trials are tests of your faith. You took on this role as leader because you had faith that you could accomplish what God has called you to do; your faith being tested proves your durability.

Every product that is put on the market for con-sumers to buy goes through tests to see how well it is made. After tweaking, some products have to go back through the same tests because of failing results and may even be taken back to the creator for corrections. When they finally pass, they are ready to go to market. The very best products cost more money and last the longest. In leadership, the wisdom to withstand the tests is what will keep you effective as a leader. This wisdom comes from God and can be obtained through prayer:

...if any of you lacks wisdom, let him ask of God, who gives to all generously and without reproach, and it will be given to him. [6] But he must ask in faith without any doubting, for the one who doubts is like the surf of the sea, driven and tossed by the wind. [7] For that man ought not to expect that he will receive anything from the Lord, [8] *being* a double-minded man, unstable in all his ways. (James 1:5-8 NASB)

Keep this in mind as you take on more responsibility: God is here, waiting for you to ask for the wisdom on how to lead your followers.

The necessity for prayer is evident through scripture, as this is a believer's connection to God.

Prayer is not a one-way conversation, for you must pray to God for revelation. How will you know what to do unless God instructs you after you pray? With thanksgiving, make your requests known to God are the instructions for prayer given in Philippians 4. The result of this kind of prayer is peace. It does not matter what is going on around you, your answer can be found in prayer. According to the website BibleGateway.com, the New American Standard Bible has 191 scriptures using the word prayer, 362 with the word pray/praying, 46 saying prayed and 6 saying prays: that is 605 references to seeking God. You will need Him that many times, and more, as a leader. Prayer is necessary to maintain open communication with God, and the Bible is not lacking in these instructions.

I vividly recall asking our congregation to pray for God to give me clarity about the vision He had for me as pastor of our church. As we prayed, God gave clarity to me and I was able to clearly communicate to the masses God's direction for our church.

God does answer prayers. You may doubt sometimes that God heard you, and on occasion, silence is the answer: but, for the most part, if you are praying regularly, you have already learned that God does answer prayers, and often the answers are swift and tangible. God heard the cries of His people in Egyptian bondage and sent Moses to deliver them; Elijah prayed for life to be restored to a woman's only child and it was done; Esther's prayers were answered to the saving of an entire nation of people; Peter was delivered from prison by miraculous means, as the saints prayed for his safe return, and many other times in scripture, you can see the intervention of a powerful God.

Prayer is one of those things that *you will* do as a believer. Jesus did not say if you pray do it this way, He said, "When you pray...." (Matt. 6:5). Prayer is a natural part of a believer's life. Why would you want to be a leader if you have no prayer life? What would be the purpose of your leadership if not to perform God's will? Just remember that Paul is recorded as saying that he prayed for deliverance from an ailment. The answer came, "My grace is sufficient for you, for power is perfected in weakness" (II Cor. 12:9, NASB). Everyone has a weakness, but God is revealed even more in him or her. When you pray, include the good, bad and your necessities.

As a preacher, there is no way to even know what to deliver in words to God's people, if not for revelation sent by God through prayer.

Chapter Two

THE POWER OF PREACHING

W hy would Paul give his son in the gospel, Timothy, instructions like this? "...preach the word; be ready in season and out of season; reprove, rebuke, exhort, with great patience and instruction...." (II Tim. 4:2, NASB). These words sound too strong for leaders just beginning in ministry. Did Paul know something that Timothy needed to learn? Paul was training him, a young man, how to lead people. His leadership would govern people of all ages; preaching the gospel of the kingdom can penetrate a life of anyone that will adhere to its power. Anyone aspiring to lead people must understand that there is power in preaching. If you can picture some of the greatest orators and feel you do not measure up because of your inexperience, you may not really know what preaching is

; the gospel carries its own weight. When you do understand and know that you can take on this role of a prepared leader, be ready in season and out of season to give a word from the gospel.

Never be afraid that you will not have a word. If you are constantly studying the Word of God and making adjustments to your own life, you have a word. There have been times when preachers received what they would say to God's people right when it was time to speak. All the scripture says is that you should be ready (II Timothy 4:2).

The purpose of preaching is to bring the Good News of the gospel to all. Preaching is beneficial in winning souls, as well as giving instructions to those who are living as born-again believers. The best attribute of preaching is that you do not have to add anything to the Word because it stands for itself. Hearing the Word of God is how you received your faith (Rom. 10:17). As a leader, it is your job to make sure your followers are maturing in their faith. You cannot just be a leader for the sake of having a title; you are in charge of believer development. They have to know the Good News of the gospel, especially that God cares about people's entire beings. It is not enough just to come to church, be an usher and sing on the praise team, or direct cars in the parking lot. People need to hear what God has said about them, and if they cannot get it from you as a leader, where else are they going to receive it?

Paul proclaimed to the Romans, "[16] For I am not ashamed of the gospel, for it is the power of God for salvation to everyone who believes, to the Jew first and also to the Greek" (Rom. 1:16, NASB). Why would Paul have to say that he was not ashamed of the gospel? It is because some people obviously were. How can you lead others and be ashamed of what you represent? This is nothing new under the sun; some would rather lead by their means and avoid conflict with those who do not know the Word. Where is this leadership taking the followers? If it is not leading them to Christ, then it is all in vain. Preaching the gospel is not just for pulpit ministry; all leaders should be equipped to encourage with what God says in the Word.

When a leader must correct a follower, the rebuke should not be made using the guidelines from your own intellect. You must understand that although someone may be late every Sunday it is her turn to teach in the nursery, it might be she may not be submitting to time management in her secular job. The correction should encourage the lady who is consistently tardy that there is also instructions to all believers to submit to those in authority, no matter where the position. She needs to understand what it says in Romans 13:1, where one power runs everything; it is the power of God. You cannot be ashamed or even afraid to preach the gospel, because *it is* the power of God.

Preaching the gospel is what gets men saved and is one of the last commandments Christ gave before His ascension into heaven: "Go into all the world and preach the gospel to all creation" (Mark 16:15, NASB). You have to remember the reason why Christ came; it was to save a lost world. Because of His life, all have the opportunity to be saved.

You are reading this because you want to be a ministry leader. What better place to preach the gospel than with a captive audience who has come to a gathering of fellow believers? You may never know what is in someone's heart, but you must always be prepared to give a word. You may be the one chosen to ignite one man's faith.

The gospel is the power of God that leads to salvation. You do not have to figure out how someone is going to develop spiritually, as your assignment is to preach what has already been written. Your job is to tell people, not to make them obey you or God. God knows how to draw people and knows how to touch their hearts. He uses people on earth to tell others about what He can do. Their awakened faith will lead them to seek God. You may be the planter or you may be the water; it does not matter because God is the one that causes His Word to grow in people's lives (I Cor. 3:7). You may have no idea where you are in the equation that represents a person's life, which is why you have to be ready to give a word. People's salvation is more important than any task that has to be completed in ministry. Learn the art of balance and develop people spiritually alongside of completing a task. That is the same course that brought you to where you are today.

The truth is that you really do not know how to lead except when God empowers you through His Word. You have watched and listened to your leaders, and gained some inside knowledge, but how this information will play out in your life is still a mystery. You sense the call to lead and the connection will come the more you preach. (Preaching is done from more than the pulpit! Preaching infers speaking forth the word of God and this can be done in a private conversation with your children, to encourage your co-worker while eating lunch or even riding on public transportation sitting next to a passenger expressing interest in salvation.) You do not have to figure out what a follower is supposed to be doing, as your life just needs to be an example. Paul, one of the greatest apostles, wrote most of the New Testament. He knew his inadequacies as a human and had no shame about alluding to the damage he had caused to believers before his conversion. Paul knew who he was to the kingdom, but refused to flaunt his authority. As great of a leader as Paul was, he said, "Be imitators of me, just as I also am of Christ" (I Cor. 1:11). He leaned on Christ as his enabler, assured of how the gospel of Christ had changed his life and preached this same gospel to those who would follow him as he followed Christ.

The power of preaching is greater than all of man's wisdom. Paul was a well-learned man, having been taught the traditions of Judaism; yet, all the knowledge and philosophies he had attained from human thinking was no match for an almighty God and the preaching of His Word. Paul was so entrenched in what *he* knew about God and His people that it took a personal, dramatic encounter with the risen Savior and blindness to get his attention (Acts 9:9). The same people whom he sought to kill had to aid him during his conversion, but it did not take long for his conversion to propel him to become one of the most profound preachers of all time.

No matter how much you believe you need to prepare to become a ministry leader, add the power of preaching to your arsenal. It is through preaching that faith is awakened, people are saved and lives are forever changed. You want to lead people that want to go, and cannot make them go along with your personality or change bad habits by your own means. This has never worked because, "…since in the wisdom of God the world through its wisdom did not come to know God, God was well-pleased through the foolishness of the message preached to save those who believe" (I Cor. 1:21, NASB). The wisdom of the world has never been able to compete against God's way of getting people to know Him.

You will always be ready if you live your life in a state of preparedness. Study the word and practice what you have learned. When opportunities come to share a word, do it; every experience that you have is preparing you for what is ahead in ministry

Chapter Three

THE POWER OF PROPER PREPARATION

There is something very intriguing about leadership. Many work diligently toward it just because they are seeking a promotion. They may even overlook some of the benefits of gathering all the information from everyday experiences that they need from being a part of the rank and file, because their goal is to become a leader. God knew that this would be somewhat of a problem for his believers. You can read it in James 3:1 Paul's warning of the believers not to readily aspire to teach. He told them that teachers will face greater judgment than other people not teaching. This section will not be a discourse on running the other way from a calling to lead or teach, but an encouragement to make sure that you are prepared when your turn comes to lead. Do not lose your enthusiasm if leading is what you desire to do; decide that you will be equipped when your name is called, because you *will* be empowered by your proper preparation from God.

While reading the above paragraph, you may have paused when the word changed from leadership to teaching. That is most likely because you may have never equated one position with the other. Of course teaching is one of the ministry gifts listed in Ephesians 4:11, but teaching is essential in each of the five listed gifts: apostles, prophets, evangelist, pastors and teachers. It makes sense if you are trying to reconcile this thought with the fact that some schoolteachers have taught for thirty years, but are buying time until retirement. This teaching position is different; in the Body of Christ, all leaders must teach. In perspective, the position of teacher in ministry is not miles apart from what is done in the public and private, primary and secondary schools across the nation, but the content of what is being taught and the character of the teacher carries a greater amount of weight.

Going to school and taking a test is all you will need in the secular arena, but ministry calls for greater, internal preparation than secular education. Leadership is teaching in ministry.

When I was first called into the ministry, at the age of sixteen, I was both nervous and excited. However, I was definitely sure of that divine call from God. I knew if I was going to be an effective leader in ministry, I had to be serious about the call that God had placed on my life. I recall many conversations that I had with my father regarding my call, and he would always tell me to pray and seek God's direction; these actions were well worth my effort and patience.

One of the fruits of the spirit is patience (Gal.5). You may have heard the word, as it relates to waiting on God to do something in your life or how you treat the less-learned. There is much more substance to this word when you align it to your life as an aspiring leader. You must learn to be patient with your process; this thought may sting, especially if you can taste your promotion coming from a mile away. However, that is a good sign that you need to work on some things in your life that could hinder your position as a leader. You must learn to be patient with your own development, for this fruit is better eaten slowly.

The greatest gift of being a believer is enjoying the journey. If you know for a fact that you have been called to lead, or you are already working in leadership, then this will be an important reading for you. All that you are learning and sharing in your walk is everything that you will need in leadership to others. The good, the bad and the ugly are parts of your process. There may come a time when a person you are leading is struggling in an area that you have already overcome. If you went through a challenge, but never stayed long enough to be delivered from the pain, this will be a stain on your character and will hinder your ability to assist someone else. An elementary school teacher may never have to worry about certain painful parts of life affecting how she teaches a child to read; but you, on the other hand, will have to constantly keep your life under the spotlight so that after leading others, your life is not lost in the shuffle. Embrace the events of your journey in preparation to leadership.

You may never have had the opportunity to attend seminary, but that does not exclude you from being a top-tier leader. What will, however, is not thinking about the preparation that your life experiences offer before you get to that point; there is power in your preparation. God does not make mistakes. The fact that you are taking your own time to read this shows that you are being chosen to either lead or support someone who will. Studying and understanding scripture will be a tool for every single step in guiding others towards their destinies. Knowing scripture and proper placement of principles is not only for the pastor, but for everyone who will have influence in the lives of believers. II Timothy 2:15 says that you are to study to show that you have been approved by God by correctly placing scriptural truths while you teach. You cannot receive this kind of knowledge without experience, and life experience cannot be taught in Bible college.

Some people have incorrectly assumed that a strong personality makes a great leader. If this were so, then Moses would have been disqualified as soon as he opened his mouth. When God told

Moses that He was sending him back to Egypt to deliver the Israelites, he complained to God about a speech impediment (Exod. 4:10). Whether Moses had a lisp (as some studies suggest) or stuttered, he felt ill-equipped to speak to a king or deliver millions of people from slavery. Someone excited about taking on a leadership role will most likely not give an excuse why he/she could not take on the responsibility, but Moses was that man. Although he had already tapped into the plight of his birth people, you never read of his strong desire to sin-glehandedly deliver them from Egypt. Instead of taking part in acquiring freedom for the Israelites, Moses had run as far away from the situation as possible. In the instructions given to him by God, he was told to allow his brother to speak on his behalf. (Exodus 7:1-2) Unfortunately, this is not the picture of someone presenting the power of personality.

Leading in God's Kingdom is a lesson in humility; you are not leading by means of per-sonality. Since birth, Moses was primed by God to lead the children of Israel out of slavery to the Promised Land. He was set up for execution by virtue of being a child born to a slave woman in

Egypt. As the Israelites were outgrowing their captors, a decree was put out to all the midwives to kill every male child born from the slaves (Num. 31:17). Disobeying the king's orders in order to obey God, the midwives saved the Hebrew boys. Moses' mother, seeing that there was something special about him, hid him for three months. When he became too big to hide, she created a tiny ark, placed her infant son in it and hid it in some brush at the edge of the Nile River. His sister, Miriam, watched as he was rescued by Pharaoh's (the king's) daughter. Miriam rushed over to Pharaoh's daughter, offering the service of her mother as caretaker of the infant. Not only was Moses nurtured by his mother until he could fully be released to his adopted family, he was reared as a prince and received a pristine education. When Moses was old enough to understand his surroundings, he was driven with compassion to see about his people.(Exodus 2:11) This would be the first show of courage and humility displayed by a man who would later lead his people to freedom.

If God had not predestined his life for leadership, Moses would have been lacking in his ability to handle the rigors of what he would eventually endure as a leader. The power of his preparation was apparent when he was saved from imminent death at birth. It was proven again as he floated down a river and providentially placed into the path of the king's compassionate daughter, only to find himself back in the arms of his loving mother who nurtured and returned him to his adoptive mother. His Egyptian education, although not mentioned as an asset, most likely assisted him in making the nine pleas to the Egyptian king for the release of God's people. (This entire story can be found in the Old Testament in the book of Exodus 1-10).

The power and preparation to lead are given by God. It is okay to desire to lead, as good leaders are always needed. The issue is not in leading but in the preparation to lead. Do not despise where you are in the process, but learn all that you can along the way. Study the process of biblical leaders, as well as the ways of those that are leading you currently. Make sure that you are a good follower. Ask yourself, am I a good worker? Have I aspired to make my leader's job easier? If you become a leader, you will have to face the same as what you see your leader facing. Learn from him/her, because the experience is part of your power of preparation.

Suffer hardship with *me*, as a good soldier of Christ Jesus. [4] No soldier in active service entangles himself in the affairs of everyday life, so that he may please the one who enlisted him as a soldier. [5] Also if anyone competes as an athlete, he does not win the prize unless he competes according to the rules. [6] The hard-working farmer ought to be the first to receive his share of the crops. (II Timothy 2:3-6, NASB)

The hardness spoken about in this passage refers to the training it takes to become a good leader. Good leaders make sacrifices. It is better to come prepared to the platform than to have to over-come inexperience. You are supposed to taste the fruit you are giving out before you ask others to eat it. You will never know whether you can handle the difficulties in ministry unless you have come through many trials.

What afflictions have you endured that equips you for leadership? What will you remember when five of your six volunteers call to say that they are not coming to help? How will you respond when the temptation to quit is overwhelming your thoughts? Did you stay in training long enough to learn all you needed? Leaders are necessary to lead God's people, as are necessary the afflictions that set them apart from those they are leading.

There is a true story of a young pastor set out to build a ministry in the back of a local day-care: his first members were he, his wife and his two small children. Every Sunday, he had to put down fold-up chairs and move the cribs out of the nursery room. When service ended, he had to put the room back in the order in which he found it. When he began to get members, it was his job to train the men to help with the set-up until the church could afford another location. He struggled with delegation and continued to work as if he were the only male member. His learning curve in delegation caused his ministry to be sluggish in congregational growth, and it took him many more years to develop a ministry that could operate without him doing everything. The suggestion here is to be aware of your flaws so that you can ask for assistance in these areas.

You must continue to be intrigued about leadership, adding to that the excitement of your passion. Yes, be passionate about learning what it takes to be a good leader. You can thrust yourself into the battle on your own, but "good" leaders are not thrown into the battle without going through extensive and intensive training. You can embrace your confidence in being able to combat all the trials and tests of leadership, but it will be the power of *proper* preparation that will enable you to stay strong. Hold onto your enthusiasm, but it will be your dependence on your godly preparation that fuels your confidence.

If you are honest with yourself, you will be confident in the things that are your strong suit. The areas where you are weak will keep you humble and enable you to be transparent with your followers. The next chapter will discuss the power of pure personality.

Chapter Four

THE POWER OF PURE PERSONALITY

In the chapter on The Power of Preparation, it was mentioned that it does not take a strong personality to be a good leader: note that this statement does not deny the influence that personality has on leadership. Personality, many times, makes all the difference in the world on whether you will become a good leader, stay a mediocre one or ever become successful as a leader. This rests on the fact that some promotions ordained by God come because of relationship. For every Bible leader that you read about, personality pronounces itself when a leader is required to make difficult decisions. God had to wrestle with some leaders to accept the duty to which they were being called and, yet, some continued to make mistakes because of their personality flaws. Everyone has personality defects, but it is the assets that overpower the personality imperfections and humility that balances them both. You may naturally have a strong personality by DNA, *or* have the propensity towards being an introvert; the call to maintain the power of pure personality will keep your leadership style in the effective zone.

There are many leadership roles; for the benefit of this writing, all leadership roles are not referring only to pastors. All ministry servants are leaders: from the pastor to the deacon's ministry leader and from the leader of the usher's ministry to the primary children's church teacher. All these roles, including others not named, need the leader to embrace the power of a pure personality. A pure personality is one not tainted with fallacies. Who God created the person to be is what will be presented to people. Of course, leadership skills must be developed, but that does not require downplaying who the person is at the core. The Bible deals with this topic in many ways. This chapter will touch on several of these scriptures, along with stories showing the personalities of some biblical leaders.

Pure is defined as not being contaminated. You may not think of a personality as having the ability to be contaminated, but it is possible. The first way that a personality gets contaminated is when people decide that they will not be who they really are; this means that they have decided that being transparent will not be part of the plan. Transparency is when you can see straight through something. When a person decides that he/she does not want people to know much about him/her, then his/her true personality is obscured. Working for someone who is just a taskmaster may work in the secular arena, where everyone is being paid or is fluffing their resumes with volunteer hours at the job. However, in ministry, you are advised to know those that work hard in ministry (I Thess. 5:12) and to respect them. This can be seen as a command from God, but it is much easier when a leader is endeared to his followers. Ministry leadership is all about people, and it is very easy to have your ministry misconstrued when you decide that the task at hand is more important than the people performing the task.

You do not have to have a weekly meeting with your staff to tell them all the sins you may have committed during the week or how rough your days have been. They are human and have the same issues. What you do, however, have to do is develop a certain care and compassion for those that desire to work side by side with you in ministry. Just as you are leading the charge to feed the homeless or creating an usher schedule for the month for ministry, the workers in charge with performing these tasks also need ministry. Some need a break and will never say anything, deciding rather to suffer in silence until they reach a breaking point. You will not know this if you are not truthful with yourself about your own needs and, therefore, more aware of the needs of others including when they may need a break. Transparency regarding your own needs and genuine concern for workers is the markings of pure personality in leadership.

Jesus told His disciples that unbelievers drive their workers with reckless abandon, but ministry leaders must be servants to their workers (Matt. 20:25-26). You have to care about how you treat your workers, because you are being watched by others outside of your manager; and if you desire the office of a pastor, you *become* the under shepherd and are watched even closer by God. It is unfortunate that many do not see the necessity of personality development as criteria for leadership, but thank God that you are reading this and will understand its place in a leadership position. If your path to leadership was created because of your faithfulness as a worker, then never forget where you came from; Continue to serve your workers as you gently guide them to accomplishing the goals of the team. On the other hand, you may have been favored immediately for leadership. Either way, it is essential that you develop the qualities of an authentic servant so that when you become a leader, you will lead with the qualities found also in your best workers.

Your personality is what sets you apart from every other human on the earth: it was developed from traits of your parents, your culture, your family dynamics, life experiences, etc. As you can see, there are many reasons why you are who you are. The previous portion of this chapter was not presented to make you believe that you have to have a complete overhaul to become a leader. Its purpose was to give you some of the traits that make your pure personality powerful. You can develop your personality away from some of the styles that may hinder your role as a ministry leader. Creating purity in your personality is not done by adding compartments to your personality, but is accomplished by removing things that block godly leadership. When you begin this process, it will not make you a clone of all ministry leaders, but will reveal who God made you to be at the core. Your personality is yours alone and there will never be another you.

Around 2013 a pastor in a southern state came to an established church when the previous pastor moved to another state. The church's second Sunday morning service began at 10:55 am, but when the pastor asked several members about the extra five minutes, he received different answers. He had inherited this practice of church service, and there was really no reason to change. Since it was a minor circumstance, he left the second service to start at 10:55am. His ego did not dictate that it be changed even though he had the authority to do that. He was trained well enough to know that the people were more important than the process. None of the members complained about the five minutes although no one seemed to remember the time of its inception. The extra five minutes remained intact.

The best part about being a ministry leader is that you have the backing of biblical guidelines to direct many of your decisions. The power in your leadership comes from the fact that you are standing on what is pure to complete your ministry calling. It is when you decide to go off script, away from the Bible, and make up rules that you run into difficulties. There are many who believe that they can lead as they go to get the job done, but the truth of the matter is the play has already been written and there is no room to add another act. The priest Eli found out the hard way that he could not allow his children to run amuck and his authority not be challenged by God, Himself (I Sam. 2). As a leader, your entire life is an example.

What do you think the people thought of Priest Eli allowing his boys to pillage through the sacrifices brought yearly to the Temple and sleep with the women working in the Temple? What the people thought, although important, was not the most important element. God was aware that Eli knew what was happening and did nothing to stop his sons. You do not have to try to figure out what God wants from you as a leader, because you have examples to follow from the Scriptures.

You cannot make the excuse that you are just like your mother or father; you may have some of their personality makeup, but you can change what is unnecessary and detrimental. Those character flaws that hinder your everyday life have a way of magnifying when you are in a leadership position. If you have a problem with patience, you may not understand the importance of not making rash decisions like Saul did in the Old Testament (I Sam. 14:24-46). Saul also had an issue with obedience. Many of you may be familiar with the story of Saul not destroying every living thing in Amalek as God instructed. The order was given because this nation gave the Hebrews a rough passage while they were on their way out of Egyptian slavery. Saul "decided" that he knew better than God, and saved the king, some sheep and whatever else he deemed was worth something in the process. However, this was not the command from God (I Sam. 15). A little obedience is still disobedience; Saul lost the kingdom because of his inability to follow instructions. God called his rebellion as evil as divination (witchcraft) (I Sam. 15:23). You cannot make your own way in ministry leadership; check your flaws and start the process of removing them. DNA will not be a worthy excuse when you are challenged to change.

Thank God for grace when you sin, for you do not want to use grace as an occasion to let your flesh lead you. The Scriptures telling you to walk by faith and not by sight are no more obvious than when you are leading God's people. God will count you faithful when you can carry out your ministry as directed by those above you or God Himself, if you are a pastor. Even as a founding pastor, you should choose to be accountable to someone. (There are too many fellowships and denominations that play The Lone Ranger card.)

It will be those small flaws in your personality that can cause you to stumble in leadership. You are going to make mistakes, but ongoing problems from your refusal to change will not be what is expected of you from God. When you do wrong, accept responsibility for it, apologize to those that your error affected and resolve not to repeat the same mistake. After that, thank God for the grace to continue leading.

In 2007 a church with five hundred members had to relocate to make room for a road the city was extending. The building where they congregated was a rental property; the church was given six months to move, so they began the process of finding a new location. When the move-out date came, they had not yet found a place within the church budget that could house the membership and thriving outreach ministries. Instead of finding a storefront building, they moved into a school. For reasons unknown to the pastor and those who remained, 425 members did not return after the first Sunday in the school. The pastor then realized that the school may not have been a good decision. He never fully understood what really happened, but his humility allowed him to continue pastoring. After a year, the pastor was able to move his dwindling congregation into a new building and begin the process of rebuilding the church body. Several members returned, without explanation, and the church went on to develop new ministries and serve the local community.

One of your largest assets in leadership is your humility; it cannot get any purer than that. Although a great leader, Elijah had the character flaw of working alone. When he ha confronted Jezebel, and killed the prophets of Baal that were serving her, she threatened to kill him (beginning in I Kings 17). Instead of rebuking the enemy and praising God that he had accomplished much of what God had sent him to do, Elijah hid and complained to God that he was the only true believer left. God corrected him and let him know that He had preserved seven thousand believers that had never bowed to Baal (the devil). What is the problem here? Elijah did not seek out wise counsel, but assumed in his own judgement that he was the only one obeying God. You are never alone. "...In the multitude of counselors there is safety" (Prov. 11:14). Surround yourself with people of wisdom. Never believe that no one will understand what you are going through; leading people is nothing new and you did not invent the wheel. There are many who have come before you and know some things, so never be too proud to ask for advice. Your humility is a sign of strength, not weakness.

Building a relationship with your ministerial workers can prove the most beneficial platform in your team. Your disconnection from the rest of the team is not how a team functions, so if you are shy or an introvert, learn how to be friendly. This attribute may not matter in the secular industry where everyone is paid, but when the majority of the workers are volunteers, your relationships make all the difference as to whether you succeed or fail in your ministry. This is when the power of a pure personality is most evident. Your team-mates do not have to be your best friends, but you must have a winning, compassionate attitude towards each member of the team. Whether or not you are a leader, showing love to your sisters and brothers is how the world knows that you are a believer (John 13:35). Since you want to lead, building a rapport with the entire team will set you all apart from many workplace teams. You will get more results if your workers like you! For those that just don't, you can still have a productive relationship on behalf of the team.

There is so much more that can be added to this topic of The Power of Pure Personality, but if you would use the principles contained in this chapter, you will be well on your way. Just know that a pure personality is not a natural thing: it takes time, patience and guidance. You cannot be afraid of rebuke. Paul wrote in Hebrews 12:6 that God chastises everyone that He loves. Think of your path to leadership as the diamond coming straight from a mine; the one-carat, beautiful diamond rings that you see were not unearthed in that form. They come out lacking any luster and must go through five different processes before reaching the jewelry store or even being set in a gold ring. (http://www.businessinsider.com/how-diamonds-are-mined-2012-8) To be chosen as one that represents the true character of an elegant, one-carat diamond, it had to hold up under the rigorous steps of purification. After this process, you can expect to pay between $3,000 and $27,000 for a one-carat diamond ring. What is your worth in ministry? Will you be an example of one who endured hardship as a leader to be rewarded with the power of pure personality?

As previously mentioned, building a good rapport with your workers is an asset along with learning to get advice from those more knowl-edgeable. This is what will be discuss in the next chapter, The Power of Partnership. On some topics you may not need outside advice if you have a partner that may have the answer you are seeking, but you will never go wrong with human resources in place.

Chapter Five

THE POWER OF PARTNERSHIP

P artnership is a very powerful entity; it is related to unity. It was mentioned in the chapter on personality that Elijah had the destructive habit of working alone. This chapter is going to assist you to get past any misconceptions that you may have about partnerships, while possibly encouraging you to join forces with others headed in your direction. You can find many passages in the Scriptures that point you to the benefits of working together. God cannot restrain Himself from answering the call from unified people. There is potent energy whenever believers come together with one heart and mind, answering the call to fulfill God's requests. Be ready for a shift in all that you do, as you add the element of partnership to what you do for the Kingdom.

Deciding to partner with someone is not handing over your personal visions and dreams to him/her, with the hope that he/she will manifest just the way God showed him/her to you. A kingdom partnership is established when two or more come together and agree on the direction of ministry, in answer to what has previously been established. John the Baptist and Jesus had two different assignments, but their partnership paved the way for what is now called Christianity. John the Baptist was given the task of preparing the way for what Jesus would do. His ministry lasted less than three years, the same length as Jesus' earthly assignment. Before it was all over, he would be beheaded (the means God allowed to end the short-lived partnership). John and Jesus' partnership was divinely appointed.

You never see John the Baptist and Jesus together except for one experience, although their ministries co-existed in history. Each one's purpose fulfilled the other's purpose, and being a forerunner of Christ made John's mission have the unique inability to coincide. The power of their partnership climaxed in one awe-inspiring moment in the Jordan River: this is the incident when Jesus comes to John to be baptized. This is the powerful culmination of two ministries coming together for one moment in time, confirming what John the Baptist had been declaring for the entire length of his ministry: "Make ready the way of the Lord" (Mark 1:3, NASB).

Every fiber of John's being must have been on alert, as Jesus came to him to be baptized in the same fashion John had done for others who believed. His mind could not contain what was taking place, and he felt inadequate to be the one who could rightfully perform such a task on the man who came to be the Savior of the world. John tried, in vain, to prevent the baptism. He said, "I have need to be baptized by You, and do You come to me?" (Matt. 3:14, NASB). Jesus explained to John that all of righteousness would be fulfilled in this one act. Immediately after Jesus arose from the water, the heavens opened and the Spirit of God descended on Him as a dove. Out of the heavens came a voice saying, "This is My beloved Son, in whom I am well-pleased"

(Matt. 3:16, NASB). This would be the beginning of the end for John's ministry.

John made all the people aware that he could only baptize them with water as a sign of their conversion, but Jesus was coming to baptize them with the Holy Ghost. You never see in scripture that John felt any less because he was not Jesus; he was assured of his calling. Because of this, there came a time when Jesus declared John the greatest man who ever lived (Matt. 11:11). Their ministries were ordained by God and played out in peace and harmony, because John knew who he was in the Kingdom and Jesus' notoriety would not downplay his assignment.

It would serve leaders well to understand this example, for there is so much more a leader can do when he/she is not standing alone. Proverbs 18:16 says, in the New American Standard Bible, that "A man's gift makes room for him, and brings him before great men." If you are bringing a gift to the Body of Christ, nobody can stop what God has ordained. You do not have to fight your way to the top or worry that someone is trying to take something from you. Use the example of John and Jesus; there was power in the Jordan River that day. Previous to the baptism, John operated in the fullness of his authority to proclaim his assignment and what Jesus was coming to do. His gift placed him before great men and his humility caused the Savior of the universe to call him great. This example of a powerful partnership can never be disputed.

The partnership that Pastor Frank Kennedy and I share is God-ordained as well. I was seeking God for an anointed, humble, gifted, articulate servant/ leader who could help me lead God's people to higher heights. I was praying and seeking God, and Pastor Kennedy was seeking God for his next assignment. The partnership we have has nothing to do with us; it was God at work in *chronos* (God orchestrated time). God providentially timed the partnership, and we have continually yielded ourselves to His hand. We have maintained the partnership through prayer, clear and constant communication, unquestionable loyalty towards one another and maintaining a servant's heart.

If your calling and election is confirmed in you, that is the conclusion of the matter. Sharing your vision with like-minded people will not hinder you from completing your task. Many have fought to the end to stand alone, to their own detriments, for the greatest ministries outlive their original leaders. When Elijah cried out in fear for his life, God pointed him to the direction of someone who would walk with him in support until he was taken up to heaven, without dying. The partnership was for an appointed time to train his successor, Elisha, as a prophet to Israel. Elisha walked with Elijah until Elijah departed this life in a whirlwind. Elisha had requested to see the miraculous departure, desiring to receive a double portion of Elijah's spirit. Elijah, secure in his ministry completion, obliged his successor. (Story can be found in I Kings 17 and II Kings 2.)

There are many stories of powerful partnerships that pronounce God's will. You can read of Paul and Silas, who were imprisoned and prayed and sang hymns together until an earthquake undid the shackles of every prisoner, including theirs, in the jail where they were being detained

(Acts 16:16-40). Moses transferred leadership to Aaron after they had been together throughout the journey of leading the Israelites out of Egyptian slavery to the Promised Land (Josh. 1:1-18). If it were not for the partnership of Jonathan to David, who would succeed Jonathan's father as king, David would likely have been killed. It does not matter that Jonathan asked for a favor for protecting David; God saw fit to put them together (I Sam. 20). There are many more stories, with all ordained by God with peaceful endings.

Ecclesiastes 4:9 (NASB) says that, "Two are better than one; because they have a good reward for their labor." Why would anyone want to remain independent when there is a guarantee of reward in a joint effort? Make the shift to add unity with other believers to fulfill a call. As long as you are humble as Jesus and John, and as assertive as Paul and Silas, your leadership will stand the test of time. Partnership takes nothing from the gift in you; it will lead you to greatness, for the power of partnership will guarantee your success.

Each example of partnership was fueled by how the two people were presented to each other. The next chapter will discuss The Power of Presentation. First impressions, although not a biblically based reason for rejection, make huge impacts on the way leaders are accepted or tolerated by their followers. Only the matured person can look past traumatic snafus and still embrace what someone has to offer.

Chapter Six

THE POWER OF PRESENTATION

There may be a misconception about how ministry leaders handle what they are presenting of themselves to other believers. Many may think that what is in leaders' hearts is more important than the way something looks or is presented by them. Unfortunately, this is far from the truth. The reason why presentation of self is so important is because people can only see the outside of leaders; God is the only one that sees into the heart. If what is being shown is not appeasing you, as the leader, the correlation of the presentation and your heart may never be understood by your audience. This also ties back into your transparency as a leader. Christian leaders need to take note of this, because they are the ones given the responsibility of leading God's people into His Kingdom. Remove the misconception and know that presentation of self is just as important as what is in your heart.

God's message of love for His people has always been the same, but there has also been a difference of how religion has been presented over the course of generations and denominations. It is a known fact that many leaders subscribe to how they were introduced to salvation and leadership when it comes to influences in their own leadership styles. Unfortunately for some, their presentation of themselves has hindered their heartfelt care of their followers. As some came up in small congregations filled with family and a few neighborhood people, they saw no need to develop a polished self to their congregants. As a result, their message was obscured by harsh criticism of lifestyle and the threat of hell to anyone whose faith had not been primed enough to change. These churches either are stagnant or saw their doors closed, as members were exposed to other ways to experience their faith during the traditional church hours on Sunday mornings and left the ministry. It may not have hindered the pastor that he/she came to know God under duress of facing hell fire, but threatening the 21st Century church by this means only does not seem to carry the weight as it once did. Although going to hell is at the center of traditional Christian teaching for non-believers, a pastor must be wise and loving in his words if he wants to be inviting to people outside of the doors of the church.

No matter what you believe, you, as a person, are attracted to what is appealing to your eyes: this applies to your natural eyes as well as your mind's eye. In order to live a disciplined lifestyle for God, a leader has to control what he/she sees. This is a good principle to apply, but you must also realize that if your desire is to draw people to what is being said or what is being shown, then it has to please both sets of eyes.

This true story of a middle-aged man who gave his life to the Lord late in life and is now an ordained minister is an example of adjusting presentation to fit the audience. He has a problem. He is an excellent leader in his church, but he wants to have the opportunity to teach and lead prayer services where he worships. He comes from a traditional Pentecostal church. The church he attends is very contemporary, and the pastor's style is inspirational with basic biblical teaching and little hoopla. The minister has no desire to change. For inspiration, he watches YouTube videos of preachers that yell and make loud noises when they inhale. When given the opportunity to teach in his home church, he mimics the preachers that he watches and not his pastor's style or the style of the other ministers in the congregation. He has no desire to change membership, but his actions are a distraction and ineffective; as a consequence, he is used infrequently. He has been mentored to make the adjustment, but he obviously believes where he received salvation and what he watches is the true way service should be conducted. There is nothing wrong with his style; it just doesn't fit in this congregation.

Power of Presentation in no way suggests that anything unnaturally pleasing to your eyes is good for nothing; the cliché, "Beauty is in the eye of the beholder," proves this relevance. What looks good to you may not look good to someone else, but there is a general consensus about presentation. One thing you know is that some things need good presentations to draw people to it. Some people will never get to the real purpose of something if they cannot see past what is being shown. Things that are not naturally beautiful, physically or mentally, will be ineffective without the extra effort of presentation.

The Bible says that to win souls, you have to be wise (Prov.11:30). There is more to achieve from winning souls than having someone repent and enter the Kingdom; a spiritual lifestyle must be developed in the person. In Ephesians 4, you can read about the calling of the apostles, prophets, teachers, evangelists and pastors: they were ordained for the "equipping of the saints, working of service and building of the body of Christ..." (Eph. 4:12, NASB). How is this ministry being presented? Are the leaders taking care to ensure that their message is reaching the right audience? Your followers need what you have to offer, so this winning in leadership takes wisdom to know The Power of Presentation.

You may recall the presentation of earlier times, when ministry leaders were taught to scare people into salvation. Going to hell was the sermon of the day. This writing is not to criticize that message, because many souls were added to the Kingdom during that era; but there are still souls left that are not inspired to change because of the fear of hell. If people were really afraid of hell, there would be more saints than sinners. There is nothing new to create, but there is a new way to present an old message. God does not desire that anyone go to hell, but He wants all to gain eternal life. What does that message look like, void of any scare tactics?

As a leader, you may not be evangelizing sinners, but you are working to help mature saints in their spirituality, as well as accomplishing the goals of your team. Just because someone came willingly into your arena does not mean that they are ready to handle large tasks with little to no errors. If you are increasing in your knowledge of how to lead people, then you must incorporate a presentation that influences your team members to take active roles in their own growth.

To know what inspires people, you must be aware of what is interesting to those you wish to engage. You may have gotten saved during the "fear" era, or you may have been raised in church and, by grace, never left. Both of those incidences are blessings, but that may not be the circumstances of your followers. Shaming someone into change may not work, although it may have worked for you. God will never leave you clueless. "In all your ways acknowledge Him, and He will make your paths straight" (Prov. 3:6, NASB). You do not have to think that you need a complete overhaul to relate to your audience. What you are doing is great; you just need to be aware that what inspires you to change may not inspire your followers.

In the book of II Kings, there came a time when Elisha's assistant needed a change in his mind's eye. Elisha was a prophet to Israel. During this particular time, the Syrian king wanted to destroy the king of Israel, but Elisha continued to give the king of Israel warnings concerning the areas he should avoid, so not to be caught. When it was made known to the King of Syria that Elisha, by way of prophecy, was thwarting his efforts, he was enraged. He sent an army to destroy Elisha.

When Elisha's servant saw the great army encircling the entire city, where they were staying, he was afraid; he did not know what to do. Elisha immediately prayed that God would open the servant's eyes so that he could see what God was doing. His faith became enlightened, and he saw horses and chariots of fire surrounding the city. Elisha then prayed for God to blind the eyes of the enemy. He was then able to lead them, in their blinded states, away from the city, as they supposedly still searched for him (II Kings 6:8-19).

This is an excellent picture of the power of presentation. If a follower is unsure or is headed in the wrong direction, a rebuke is not always the answer. If you were a faithful follower, you would believe that you have picked up on some of the ways of your leader, especially in the attributes of walking by faith. Gehazi, Elisha's servant, had been with Elisha when he raised a dead boy to life, healed a king of leprosy, purified poisonous stew, miraculously fed one hundred men and made an iron ax head float, but yet he doubted when seemingly faced with insurmountable odds (II Kings 4-6). This is the difference between a leader and a follower. As a leader, you are to paint a picture of what following God looks like. Yes, God does rebuke, but is every "offense" worthy of a rebuke? Or, can you think of a better way to teach faith through the power of a God-inspired presentation, like what Elisha did?

Leaders are given the responsibility of equipping the people of God with correction and encouragement. Just because you may be spiritually ten steps ahead of your team, that is no excuse to be intolerant of their positions. The evidence of where they are shows how they respond to certain circumstances. When they show you their spiritual immaturity, do not be quick to rebuke or cause them to draw back because of the way they are treated. Gently guide them closer to where you are by using persuasive demonstrations in the way you talk and your demeanor towards them. Training takes time, and it is the leader's responsibility to enable the followers to grow.

The very person that you decide is not growing fast enough may need just one more presentation to prove that he/she is your next great team leader. God uses things that appear foolish to some just to shame the wise (I Cor. 1:27); be careful because he/she may be the one God is empowering to lead your outreach ministry.

Chapter Seven

THE POWER OF PROVIDENTIAL PLACEMENT

G od rules over everything; His sovereignty can be seen in every facet of existence, animate and inanimate. Whether you can see it or not, it is still governed by God. His purpose is being established, and His will is going to be established. Psalm 103:19, in the New American Standard Bible, states it like this: "The LORD has established His throne in the heavens, and His sovereignty rules over all." He puts up leaders and takes down kings. Providential placement is a reality, and there is nothing man can do to thwart the efforts of an all-powerful God. No matter how anyone may believe in human control or some other underlying workings, God directs it all.

If you are looking for God's hand being involved, all you have to do is look throughout history and scripture, and see how He orchestrated the placement of leaders to do great exploits. David was tending to his father's sheep when God sent Samuel to David's family to anoint a new king. His father, Jesse, presented his other seven sons as the possible next king. God told Samuel that none of them were who He was looking for, which ultimately lead Jesse to have to answer Samuel's request about another son. He called shepherd David from out of the field; he was anointed right then and there, wearing whatever it was he had on from working with the animals. God's hand is in all. He is conducting every area so that His will can be done.

Unlike some people, God covers some of the worst sins to use many people in His plan. He called King David, "a man after my heart" (Acts 13:22, NASB): David, the king who had slept with another man's wife and then had that same man killed. (See II Samuel 11.) No matter where you are or what you have done; God can still call you to lead His people. He knew that

David would do His will. Never think of yourself as not being worthy of God's call. If you sense the call of God on your life for ministry leadership, answer it; you are equipped when you step out. God's Holy Spirit will empower you to carry out your call. Who God calls, He also justifies and glorifies (Rom. 8:30). David wrote this about believers, "…How blessed is he whose transgression is forgiven, Whose sin is covered!" (Ps. 32:1, NASB). Not only does God forgive sins, He uses who He wants to accomplish His will.

You cannot determine the right place and right time for God's call. It may be the most in-opportune time or it may be right at the moment that you were expecting. "The thoughts of God no one knows except the Spirit of God" (I Cor. 2:11, NASB). You do not know how God moves, but He sends His message by way of the Holy Spirit. If He is calling you, you *will* know. It is so much easier to operate when the hand of the Lord is on you, because time is in God's hands. You cannot decide when your time is, or whether you feel you are ready. You will be equipped when He calls you.

Ask Paul, who was one of the main persecutors of all believers. He had just received letters to go to the city of Damascus, authorizing him to arrest all those believing in Jesus and have them sent to Jerusalem. Believers were afraid of him. On his journey there, the risen Savior, Jesus Christ Himself, arrested him. Rebuked and made blind, he needed someone to lead him to the very city where he was originally going to do damage, but would now be a place for the completion of his change. A believer by the name of Ananias had to be assured that Paul was coming as a new man; and he was going to be the one to pray for Paul to receive his sight and be filled with the Holy Spirit (Acts 9:17). He was told, directly from Jesus, that Paul was a chosen vessel to preach: "Go, for he is a chosen instrument of Mine, to bear My name before the Gentiles and kings and the sons of Israel;" (Acts 9:15, NASB). What a change from how Paul first started out. It would be in this same city where he would st art preaching and declaring that Jesus is Lord. He was called from a lead persecutor to a disciple of the risen Savior.

Going to Jerusalem would not be as easy. Although the people of Damascus were astonished at Paul's conversion and still afraid of him, they did not retaliate for his previous actions. However, the Jews in Jerusalem were not as easy to be won over by his sudden change. The disciples had to be persuaded of what had been done. Barnabas was God's chosen partner for this time in Paul's life. He convinced the disciples of Paul's experience and real conversion; yet, there were still many Jews who wanted him killed because he was now the enemy of those whose beliefs against Christ he had previously supported (Acts 9:29). Stepping up into new ministry leadership is not always going to be easy. You may not be facing the threat of death, but you may face persecution. Providential placement says one great thing, if it says nothing else, "...If God is for us, who is against us?" (Acts 9:31b, NASB). It may not be easy, but submitting to God will be more than worth it.

God called Gideon, in Judges 6, to lead the Israelites against the mighty army of the Midianites. Where did God find Gideon: threshing wheat in the wine press, trying to hide it from the enemy. Gideon did not see himself as a great leader; he went back and forth with God, asking for proof in several different ways. Here God is calling him, and he is *telling God* that his family is the least in their city and he is the youngest. This is his response to God calling him a valiant warrior (Judg. 6:12). God promised to be with Him; now, many of you are not any different than this. God says go, and you tell Him why you cannot. This is the point of the power of providential calling. God enables those He is calling to act. If He knew that you were not able, you would not be called. God gets the glory out of using the least likely and most reluctant. God calls whomever He desires.

God used Esther, a previous orphan, to be favored by a king who would have carried out the massacre of the Jews in answer to one of his leaders' complaints. Esther's providential place-ment could not have come at a better time. The king loved her so much he would have given her half of his kingdom if she so desired. He had not known her heritage, but God fixed it so that Esther would conceal this fact until the time that its significance would make the greatest impact for the saving of her people. Living with such great favor, of which she most likely had never felt previously, she was at first reluctant to talk to the king on behalf of her people. Being compelled by her uncle, Mordecai, he asked;

For if you remain silent at this time, relief and deliverance will arise for the Jews from another place and you and your father's house will perish. And who knows whether you have not attained royalty for such a time as this? (Esther 4:14, NASB)

It was against the law to go to the king, unless he called for you; nonetheless, her uncle's wisdom compelled her to take the risk, seeing that her heritage would have most likely excluded her from the pageant that boosted her into the palace. Fasting, praying and calling on the confidence in herself from her God, she proclaimed, "I will go in to the king, which is not according to the law; and if I perish, I perish" (Esth 4:16, NASB).

God designs your placement; know that He is in full control and makes no mistakes. If He sends you, He can keep you. You do not have to jockey for position, because He knows where and when to use you. Ministry leaders are always needed. The Word says that, "the harvest is plentiful, but the workers are few" (Matt. 9:37, NASB). This is the harvest of souls; there has never been, and never will be, a shortage of sheep. Where are the good leaders? There is always a need. Submit to the calling and accept The Power of Providential Placement

Making hard decisions is sometimes painful; emotional pain makes the results of God's calling worth it that much more. As you continue to read, you will see that there is also power in your pain.

Chapter Eight

THE POWER OF PAIN

If you are like average people, the thought of any power that can be perceived in pain is lost in saying the word pain. However, pain sounds like something else when you put God in the middle of it. If you study the lives of many of the Bible greats, you will see hardship, pain, trouble and then God's intervention. Psalm 34:19 (NASB) says it this way: "Many are the afflictions of the righteous, But the Lord delivers him out of them all." The key word here is *many*. There is a price for walking with the Lord and doing His will. Salvation is free, but stepping up to obey His call has a cost. God gets the glory out of every situation that cannot be victorious without Him. There is power in your pain. To fulfill your destiny, accept the afflictions that come with the territory. You will see the power in your pain if you endure it.

Paul talks about boasting in his weaknesses, so that Jesus Christ's power can rest on Him. (II Cor. 12:9). Boast is a rather strong word to use when you are talking about pain and weakness. You will have a different perspective after you have suffered and experienced God's deliverance. This is not a one-time consequence for following God's plan for your life. You are regularly impeding on the enemy's territory, as you expand the Kingdom of God. When you take on that position of leader in the expansion of the Kingdom, you have to expect war. Jesus said that, "From the days of John the Baptist until now the kingdom of heaven suffers violence, and violent men take it by force" (Matt. 11:12, NASB). John the Baptist proclaimed the coming of the Kingdom before Jesus' ministry began. Jesus upped the warfare by dying on the cross and giving the power of the Holy Spirit to all believers, not just to dwell among you, but to also live in you. Do you think that the enemy is going to stand by and let the earth be covered with the glory of God? He did not even let Adam and Eve enjoy the beautiful place of the Garden of Eden without interfering in God's plan for mankind. Yes, boasting in your dependence on Jesus Christ is your best defense.

Joseph, in the Old Testament, was a dreamer. He was the youngest child and favored by his father. He dreamed of ruling over his entire family, including his mother and father. His brothers evidently believed it, because they plotted to fake his death, but later decided to sell him into slavery. They believed that they could change the course of their little brother's life, by sending him away from his family and familiar surroundings. They did not understand that, "A man's gift makes room for him, and brings him before great men" (Prov. 18:16, NASB). His ability to dream and interpret became a gift.

This was not even close to the end of Joseph's hardship. He was sold as a slave to the king of Egypt. With favor resting on him, he was easily promoted to top servant in the king's house, but trouble continued to follow him. The king's wife made advances on him, causing him to run out of the house. When the king returned home, his wife told him that Joseph had tried to rape her; Joseph was thrown in jail because of it. (Genesis 39:20)

Throughout this entire period, God's hand still guided Joseph's affairs. In prison, he was promoted by the warden to run everything in the prison; God was still at work, planning the use of Joseph's gifts. The king's cupbearer and baker did something to offend the king and ended up in the same prison with Joseph. They were put under the care of Joseph. One night they both had dreams, but had no way of understanding what either dream meant. Joseph discerned their consternation and asked what was wrong. Sharing their dreams with Joseph was the beginning of things turning around in Joseph's favor. Joseph gave God glory, telling them both that interpretations belong to God. (You see, the bragging he did about God's power.) He was empowered by God to give meanings to their dreams. The baker's dream showed that he would be sentenced to death, but the cupbearer's dream relayed a message of restoration to his previous position. Joseph asked the cupbearer to remember him and relay his story; this plan would have worked well for Joseph, except for the fact that Joseph's full elevation was still being prepared by God. (Genesis 40:5-23)

After being freed, the cupbearer forgot about Joseph and his request. Two full years would past before God's plan for Joseph's life would unfold. Pharaoh, the king, had two dreams that troubled his spirit: the king's first dream was about seven fat cows and then seven skinny cows; his second dream was about seven healthy ears of grain and continued with seven scorched ears of grain. After calling for all the magicians and wise men of Egypt, none of them could interpret the dreams. It was then that the cupbearer recalled Joseph's request and gift of dream interpretation.

Joseph was cleaned up and sent to tell the king what the dreams meant. (His gift was standing him before great men.) Once again, giving God glory, he said that, "It is not in me; God will give Pharaoh a favorable answer" (Gen. 41:16, NASB). (Here it is again, boasting about God's authority and not his own!) The dreams meant that Egypt would be plunged into a famine after having seven prosperous years of harvest. He also told the king that he needed to find a man who could manage the prosperous years, ensuring that grain would be left for the years of lack. The king could think of no one other than Joseph to fill this position; Joseph was given charge over every province in Egypt. The king was the only person with more authority. His gift of interpreting dreams had finally given him promotion.

As the seven plenteous years came and went, the famine became great in the land. It reached Canaan, where Joseph's family resided. His entire family ended up having to come to Egypt and coming before Joseph to request food to help them survive the famine. Joseph's original dream was being played out; the family had to submit to Joseph in order to live. At this time Joseph promised to provide for them and they stayed in Egypt for the rest of their days. (Story can be found in Genesis 39-50.)

There was power in Joseph's pain. What lesson should you learn from Joseph's life? You should understand how to suffer as a good soldier in God's Kingdom. Joseph went through the pain of slavery, prison and a dream deferred just for the sake of God's glory. You have to believe that Joseph may have even doubted, at some point, how his dream would pan out. When would he fulfill his call to have authority over his family? If he did suffer mentally because of his plight, the Scriptures make no mention of it. A good soldier does not complain; he just holds onto hope of what was promised. He does not want to die before tasting what God said. King David wrote in, "I would have despaired unless I had believed that I would see the goodness of the LORD In the land of the living" (Ps. 27:13, NASB). No matter what circumstances look like, you have to believe what God said. The power of Joseph's pain was evident in how he expressed himself throughout his dilemma, believing what God said during his trying times.

When Joseph first dreamed, in Genesis 37, he was elated to tell his brothers and father that he would rule over them. His dream was expressed in such a way that his brothers and father knew that the interpretation meant that he would have authority over them. As painful circumstances began to enter Joseph's life, he softened his tone. He told the cupbearer, baker and the king of Egypt that God gave interpretations of dreams. You do not see these words said when he was a teenager, the youngest child being spoiled by his daddy. God knows how to humble and test you, and show what is in your heart to see if you will obey Him (Deut. 8:2 NASB). He used this same method for the children of Israel in the wilderness; it took forty years to humble them, while Joseph's painful journey took thirteen years. You may see greatness in your future, but consider how you share it, knowing that God sets things for an appointed time and some testing is sure to come.

There was a time when I was waiting for God to give me my next assignment. Some people were giving me advice about what I should do, but I was waiting on God to give me my assignment. It was painful enduring well-intentioned individuals trying to push me where God was not leading me. However, I knew God had promised an assignment that would be both fruitful and fulfilling for my life as a servant/ leader. Although painful, it was well worth the wait to serve a congregation that was both loving and compassionate.

As a leader in God's Kingdom, you have been presented with a tremendous responsibility. You cannot afford to think that it will be smooth sailing, but know that there will be pain and you have to be patient. If you noticed no other fruit from Joseph's life, you cannot deny that he was extremely patient. He was given a vision, but it would take God thirteen years to allow it to come to pass. God is God, so that dream could have been manifested at any time, but Joseph's testing and humbling took time. God knows already what is in you and what it is going to take for you to be developed to fulfill the call on your life. You may already be operating in your call, but God is never through with you. You have people that are watching you. You are not just given an opportunity to look great by having people follow you. God's people are very important to Him and your responsibility cannot be taken lightly.

When you see your assignment clearly, you may want to keep it to yourself because the pain that may come to you can dim your vision. You may even have a time of doubting. Through your pain, hold on to what God has spoken to you through dreams, visions or prophecies. No matter where Joseph found himself, he never forgot what he saw. This is an excellent principle to keep in mind, because it will cover you while you work to reach your destination. The pain is a platform to your power.

Joseph had thirteen long years of pain, but in the end, it was all worth it. The king knew to sustain his kingdom he needed a person who could administrate what was about to happen to his land and the areas around him. He promoted Joseph, but it took nothing away from his authority; in fact, it showed his confidence in his ability as king. It took Joseph thirteen years to realize his elevation, but it only took the king a moment to know whom to promote.

Chapter Nine

THE POWER OF PROMOTING

Y ou may have heard it in conversations on the airwaves or talked about it with your peers. The subject matter is the concept of promoting people. This is a very important principle for leaders who know what God has given them to do, as a leader is much bigger than them. For great projects, there is no way for one person to do everything that is required to make the project successful. In the story of Joseph, from the previous chapter, the king had no issue with promoting a prisoner; you can see this played out throughout the Bible. Even God, Himself, employed people to carry out what He wants done in the earth. Jesus' death, burial and resurrection promoted man to do greater works than Jesus (John 14:12, NASB). When one plan has reached its maximum effectiveness, you see God adding to it by promoting people. This subject is worth implementing when you understand what to do and when it should be done.

Moses, as God instructed, had the immense task of leading millions of people out of slavery to the Promised Land. The people were safely out of Egyptian slavery and on their way to their homeland, Israel; it was a daunting task. With millions of people and Moses, no doubt, handling all the problems alone, his father-in-law, Jethro, one day pulled him aside and said, "The thing that you are doing is not good. [18] You will surely wear out, both yourself and these people who are with you, for the task is too heavy for you; you cannot do it alone" (Exod. 18:17,18, NASB). One of the most important points to see here is that Moses was not only going to burn himself out; he was going to wear out those he was charged with leading to safety in the Promised Land. Sometimes in the middle of the task, you may not see how crucial it is to delegate some authority. You may naturally be a workaholic, but that does not give you an excuse to wear down your followers. At some point, this kind of work ethic is not going to work for you either. God knows the task is too big for you, and He expects you to train and promote others that can duplicate what you have been given to do.

What Moses was doing could not continue. He wanted each of his followers to understand the Law. He spent countless hours putting out fires and resolving simple disputes, which could last well into the night. If you have a family with children that you are in charge with caring for, imagine, in your life, Moses' task multiplied thousands of times over. This is exactly what Moses was doing alone. When this kind of activity continues, the team will suffer. Others who may also have leadership potential will know that they have to be cleared through Moses before any decision was made.

What happens in this situation is that the leader minimizes what *needs* to be done. Needs do not get met and God's full plan is never fully done; the very thing that the leader thinks that he is avoiding is taking place. The leader believes he is the only one that can serve everyone, but being only one person many may go neglected. What the leader can manage gets to be more important than the entire scope of what God wants for His people. In a shortened version, this is called micro managing. This is not a good principle in the secular arena, but more so in the spiritual arena when people are coming for spiritual guidance. There had to be a change for Moses.

Moses heeded the instructions of Jethro to, "...select out of all the people able men who fear God, men of truth, those who hate dishonest gain" (Exod. 18:21, NASB). The only stipulation was that the harder issues were to be brought to Moses, but the daily task of judging between right and wrong was charged to able-bodied men. Moses still taught the people from the Law, but the daily operations were delegated out. There was no way that the completion of what God said could have been sufficiently followed with a man that wanted to handle everything. Jethro stood as a leadership consultant. Moses did not have the luxury of living in ego, as it was to the detriment of the entire wilderness excursion.

What God asks of His leaders is always bigger than what one person can do. As you accept the call on your life for leadership, you do well to take note of the teachings on promoting people. When you empower people to make decisions without your constant input, you lessen your load, expand your sphere of influence and ensure that what God is requiring is being done. This is the platform of great companies and even greater ministries; this way will never go out of style.

One important aspect of what Moses did was to promote faithful men to rule over the amount of people that they had the ability to handle. Jethro suggested and Moses complied, placing men over "thousands, of hundreds, of fifties and of tens" (Exod. 18:25, NASB). Everyone cannot handle the same load; we are created the same, but are given different roles to fulfill our destinies. If you do not delegate responsibly, you will cause the same issue that you are trying to avoid: all duties not being fulfilled. There will never be a shortage of God's people, His sheep, but those that are shepherding are few. Jesus took note of this when He told His disciples: "The harvest is plentiful, but the workers are few. Therefore, beseech the Lord of the harvest to send out workers into His harvest" (Matt. 9:38, NASB). The workers must be given duties over people based on what they can handle effectively.

Besides doing the work of the ministry with people, there are many other things in ministry that need to be done. You may be a marketing guru, but if you are the one leading people, making the big decisions and delegating authority, it serves you well to seek out others that can understand what you are requesting and pro-duce results equal to your expectations. If you are really seeking to please God, you will not have time alone to fulfill every aspect of the vision entrusted to you by God. When you begin to per-fect delegation, teach it to others who can follow your lead. Supervising people and doing admin-istrative duties are two of the things that ministry require. God knew this when He gifted people to accomplish the organizational duties.

You must be careful not just to promote people out of necessity, without really knowing who they are and what they have proven they can do. One way that God handles giving out more respon-sibilities is to see if a person has taken care of small things first. In Luke 16:10, it says, "He who is faithful in a very little thing is faithful also in much...." (NASB). Unless someone comes recommended to you with a highly decorated resume, start with small tasks for the person. Even with a resume, every ministry is different. The Great Commission is the same for everyone, but how that is handled in your ministry may be different. Small tasks that are completed in a timely fashion, and to your expectations, may be just the element you're looking for in a person to run a project under your domain.

The scripture from I Timothy 5:22 that reads not to be quick to lay hands on someone often has been misinterpreted. Because of the misunderstanding, some have said that ministers should be careful who they lay hands on, even when praying for the sick. This verse is actually referring to the ordaining of leadership. The entire passage, beginning at the verse 17 says that elders in the ministry who do well are worthy of double honor. By the time the passage reaches verse 22, there is an admonition to be careful of promoting those who may have carnal issues. Promoting them will cause more problems for your ministry and you will share in their sins. You are not going to start judging potential assistants by what appears, but by what you know. It will be well for you to understand this and not cause undue hardship on what you are trying to accomplish. God will send what you need, and you will praise God for your understanding of this scripture.

Promoting others is probably one of the easiest entities of leadership: "For not from the east, nor from the west, Nor from the desert comes exaltation...." (Ps. 75:6, NASB). What this verse is saying is that God alone has the authority to promote. If that is the case, you need to know your strategy in promoting people. Remember the scripture in Matthew 9:38, instructing you to pray to God for laborers? God not only hears those prayers, but He also answers; He wants His will done in the earth. As you become successful in leadership, you will see the need to promote. Giving others a portion of your leadership takes nothing from you. The more effective your leadership, the more God will send those that will be promoted. The principle also applies to you about being faithful over a few things and given more to do. It will be harder for you not to promote if you are leading the masses individually.

All authority is God's authority. God establishes every delegated authority (Rom. 13:1, NASB). If you are a leader, this dynamic has been ordained by God; as God redeemed the world from the hands of the enemy by sending His only son, Jesus, to die for your sins, He also empowered people to do great works after Jesus ascended back to Him (John 14:12). The greatest leaders are those that understand servanthood. As you serve people, you never want anyone to be neglected; this is where Moses was headed. People need and desire to be led. When your ministry expands, so will your need to promote. Do not allow the sheep to be led astray by attempting to do everything on your own. Promoting takes nothing away from you, but shows your true heart and desire to see God's will performed. The power to lead and promote both comes from a loving Savior.

You may never fully understand the concept of promotion until you begin to promote others.

You have seen examples from scripture and you can ask others in authority how it works. You will know the power of promotion when you heed the call from God to promote. Because promotion does not come from man, you will not be confused when you are presented with a candidate. Understanding will come when you obey the call to promote.

One of the best steps that will allow you freedom in promoting is when you plan. When you have sat down and begun writing and meeting with others about your next, big undertaking, you will see the need for other workers to join forces with you. Planning is one of the most effective tools you will use as a leader.

Chapter Ten

THE POWER OF PLANNING

No one that wants to be successful in ministry steps out to do great feats without first planning. Although you will never be able to see everything that you are up against until it appears, there are basic guidelines to follow that will make your assignment flow better. You can pray and fast, hoping that things work out, but your decision to plan will make the greatest impact on your ministry. God is not to be taken out of the equation, but He wants you active and most activities work best when they are planned. Do not take for granted that you are smart enough to make changes as you go, because even God gives clear instructions on where He says to go. God knows the benefits of planning.

God told Moses how to save the Hebrew male children from the final plague sent on Egypt on its refusal to let the people go. He sent clear and precise instructions about the sacrifice that would cause the death angel to pass over their homes (Exod. 12:7). God knows how to get you through difficult times as well as prosperous times. Without acknowledging God for direction, you may fail. Thank God for grace, but why take it for granted when you can ask for directions? "In all your ways acknowledge Him, and He will make your paths straight" (Prov. 3:6, NASB). "Commit your works to the Lord and your plans will be established" (Prov. 16:3, NASB). You can find, throughout scripture, encouragement to get God involved in what He is instructing you to do. God has a plan to get you around the greatest of obstacles, but you have to ask and expect an answer.

If you start your ministry without a plan, you cannot blame God when it is not successful. Scripture tells you to count up the cost: you need to know how much time, effort, people, space, etc., you will need to bring your vision to frui-tion. You cannot assume that everything will just fall into place. When you have laid the founda-tion, and cannot go any further, whose fault is that? When God wanted to use Law to direct His people, He gave the Ten Commandments to Moses on Mount Sinai (Exod. 20). They were specific instructions on how the people should live and worship God. The word-plan means detailed instructions for doing and achieving something. Where in that definition do you see any room for contrived behavior? You have to stay close enough to God so that you can hear the plan all the way through to the end before you get started.

It is popular now to tell people just to start doing something; this is not scriptural nor is it God's desire for you to fail. When He appoints you to a duty, He expects you to be able to carry it all the way until its ending. Saul was dethroned as the first King of Israel, because of his inability to follow instructions given by God, by way of His prophets (I Sam. 15). God had a plan for His people. His authority to be king was not taken away because God did not know what to do with His people. God knows that His instructions will accomplish *His* ultimate plan to the highest degree. When you do not either follow instructions or have not heard them, you are ill-prepared to lead. When

Moses was leading the children of Israel through the wilderness, there were times when he had to stop because a glory cloud rested above them. When it lifted, they could continue their journey (Exod. 40:36). God knows well how to lead His people. He will send circumstances to tell you when to start and times when it is time to wait.

When Moses had just led the people out of slavery, they came to the Red Sea; crossing a sea obviously seemed like an impossible task. During the previous period, Moses had spent countless hours with God, receiving instructions on how to deal with a hard-hearted king. God promised to deliver His people, and that is what He was doing, but the Red Sea made the people panic. Moses decided to take this time to let the people know that God would deliver them. Moses did not know how God was going to accomplish this when right in front of them was a great body of water. God did not allow Moses to do what he thought was best. As Moses was making his speech about not seeing these enemies again, God stopped him right then and said:

> Why are you crying out to Me? Tell the sons of Israel to go forward. [16] As for you, lift up your staff and stretch out your hand over the sea and divide it, and the sons of Israel shall go through the midst of the sea on dry land. (Exodus 14:15-16 NASB)

If God gives you a task, He is well able to see you through it. Not even the Red Sea could stop plans given by God.

When Pastor Davidson asks me to implement new and innovative ideas for ministry, I have had to spend time planning. The process is both prayerful and methodical. Because Pastor Davidson and I have been divinely connected, I have had to take the time to strategically plan how the other ministry workers and I would collectively facilitate the pastor's vision. Also, a part of that process was seeking God for the right individuals to support and the time to implement the plan. In particular, Christian Education and Evangelism have been two areas where planning has been of paramount importance. My connection with

Pastor Davidson has made my plans coincide with his vision for the ministry.

Never get caught up in what you think; your ways and thoughts are not like God's. He knows how to direct everything you do. As a leader, you have to be very careful to listen for God's instructions. God had already told Moses that the children of Israel would be delivered, but he probably did not have a clue of what God had intended for the crossing of an ocean. Sometimes all you will have is your faith to connect you with God. You may not have a clue of how God is going to accomplish what He is telling you to do. What you do have to do is hear His voice and follow His instructions. He guarantees to hear the cries of His people; never get too confident to ask for help. He told you what to do, but you are not sure how it is going to work. At least you have a plan. God wants you to make plans from what He puts in your hearts, but He also wants you to know that bringing them to fruition is His job. "The mind of man plans his way, But the LORD directs his steps" (Prov. 16:9, NASB). No matter what *you* think, God knows *the* way.

Planning takes time and patience. If you do not submit your plans to the Lord, you may end up wasting resources and time. Saul made a hasty oath because he did not wait for guidance (I Sam. 14). His impatience caused a string of unnecessary hardships on his people. When circumstances caused his plans not to produce his desired result, his intolerance did not allow him to see his own errors; this is a sign of weak leadership. When you can admit to weakness is when you become strong. The great apostle Paul said, "For I determined to know nothing among you except Jesus Christ, and Him crucified" (I Cor. 2:2, NASB). If you know anything about Paul, you know that he wrote most of the New Testament. With all that Paul had endured, it humbled him to the point of his resolve to know nothing but Jesus Christ and His crucifixion. This great apostle "decided" to rest on the simple Gospel of Jesus Christ. He could have used his intellect and talked from a lofty perspective, but the fabric of his life molded from trials, including stoning and many imprisonments, rendered him humbled. You do well to learn from this example; Saul is a model of what not to do. No matter how intellectual you are or how great you perceive your wisdom to be, planning takes time and patience.

God desires and gives strategic plans. You can see examples of leaders that carried out God's instructions with excellence. Noah had never seen rain, yet God gave him instructions, down to the minutest detail, to build an ark that would save his family from a flood. (Genesis 5:32-10:1) Nehemiah's desire was to see the wall of Jerusalem rebuilt. With a plan and a heart to work, the job was completed in fifty-two days. (Nehemiah 6:15-19) King David wanted to build a temple to the Lord, but his hands had known too many wars. He gave the Temple plans to his successor, his son Solomon, who built a temple that manifested all that David had imagined. (II Chronicles 3) Planning did not stop in the Old Testament. Jesus spoke of a wise man that built his house on a rock and it withstood all matter of weather changes; and then there is the foolish man who built his house on sand and when streams rose and winds blew, the house was destroyed because it had no foundation (Matt. 7).

Jesus was an ultimate planner. He hid when His enemies came to destroy Him before time, and He confidently spoke of fulfilling his mission:(-John 8:59; Luke 24:44-49)

Just at that time some Pharisees approached, saying to Him, "Go away, leave here, for Herod wants to kill You." [32] And He said to them, "Go and tell that fox, 'Behold, I cast out demons and perform cures today and tomorrow, and the third *day* I reach My goal.'" (Luke 13:31-32, NASB)

Are you prepared to say you will reach your goals because you know how important it is to plan?

There is power in planning; God expects you to plan and He expects you to trust Him to make the plans work. You never take God out of the equation, but His wisdom is the principle thing. He wants you to rest on His strategies. You should not ever be afraid to make mistakes, for mistakes are the best teachers of better planning. When you have taken on your role as leader, and have been given your orders to move forward, remember to recognize God's involvement. This is the secret in the power of planning:

Unless the LORD builds the house, They labor in vain who build it; Unless the LORD guards the city, The watchman keeps awake in vain. [2] It is vain for you to rise up early, To retire late, To eat the bread of painful labors; For He gives to His beloved *even in his* sleep. (Psalms 127: 1-2)

Your best planning will come when you know who is doing the building.

Conclusion

TAKING THE CALL

This book, although condensed, is the result of fifty-five years of combined ministry of Pastors Marcus Davidson and Frank Kennedy Jr. The information contained herein could not have been displayed if it had not been for our years of experience. Every step has not always transitioned without a difficulty, but God's grace has always been there to sustain what He has ordained.

May God grant you the peace and wisdom you will need, as you gather all the information to be an effective ministry leader. Wisdom is the proper application of knowledge. Learn all that you can and pray about everything. God's wisdom will direct you how to apply all that you have learned so that you will be a blessing to His people.

Recall that the harvest is ripe and workers are few (Matt. 9:37, NASB), as you walk towards your destiny in God. He is always in search of willing leaders to guide His sheep. Someone is praying for you to take the assignment for which you have been called. Your experiences and godly wisdom has equipped you for where God is sending you. God anoints those that He appoints with the Power of Leadership.

ABOUT THE AUTHORS

Marcus D. Davidson is married to Yvokia and they have one daughter, Layla Alexandria. He serves as pastor of the New Mount Olive Baptist Church, Fort Lauderdale, Florida. He holds degrees from Alabama Agricultural and Mechanical University, Samford University, and The Southern Baptist Theological Seminary.

Frank Kennedy Jr. is married to Denise and they have two daughters, Cierro and Lachastity. He serves as Executive Pastor of the New Mount Olive Baptist Church, Fort Lauderdale, Florida. He holds degrees from Samford University.